Radford Public Library
30 First St.
Radford, VA 24141

P9-CQE-746

HUSH!

A Thai Lullaby

by

MINFONG HO

pictures by

HOLLY MEADE

Orchard Books
New York

Text copyright © 1996 by Minfong Ho

Illustrations copyright © 1996 by Holly Meade

All rights reserved. No part of this book may be reproduced
or transmitted in any form or by any means, electronic or
mechanical, including photocopying, recording, or by any
information storage or retrieval system, without
permission in writing from the Publisher.

Orchard Books
95 Madison Avenue
New York, NY 10016

Manufactured in the United States of America
Printed by Barton Press, Inc.   Bound by Horowitz/Rae
Book design by Chris Hammill Paul

10   9   8   7   6   5   4   3   2   1

The text of this book is set in 19 point Weiss.
The illustrations are cut-paper collage with ink.

Library of Congress Cataloging-in-Publication Data

Ho, Minfong.
        Hush! : a Thai lullaby / by Minfong Ho ; pictures by
Holly Meade.
        p.   cm.
        Summary: A lullaby which asks animals such as a lizard,
monkey, and water buffalo to be quiet and not disturb the sleeping
baby.
        ISBN 0-531-09500-2. — ISBN 0-531-08850-2 (lib. bdg.)
        1. Thailand—Juvenile poetry. 2. Lullabies, American.
[1. Thailand—Poetry. 2. Lullabies. 3. American poetry.]
I. Meade, Holly, ill. II. Title.
PS3558.0316H87   1996
811'.54—DC20   95-23251

For my father, Ho Rih Hwa,
whose wonderful bedtime stories of
giants and turtles,
elephants and warriors would
leave me more wide-eyed than sleepy,
when I was a little girl growing up
in Thailand —M.H.

For Annie Elizabeth and Kevin James,
with love —H.M.

Hush!
Who's that weeping
in the wind?

"Wee-wee, Wee-wee,"
A small mosquito.

Mosquito, mosquito,
don't come weeping.
Can't you see that
Baby's sleeping?
Mosquito, mosquito,
don't you cry,
My baby's sleeping
right nearby.

Hush!
Who's that peeping
from the ceiling?

"Tuk-ghaa, Tuk-ghaa!"
A long-tailed lizard.

Lizard, lizard,
don't come peeping.
Can't you see that
Baby's sleeping?
Lizard, lizard,
don't you cry,
My baby's sleeping
right nearby.

Hush!
Who's that creeping
under the house?

"MEOW, MEOW,"
A lean black cat.

Black cat, black cat,
don't come creeping.
Can't you see that
Baby's sleeping?
Black cat, black cat,
don't you cry,
My baby's sleeping
right nearby.

Hush!
Who's that squeaking
by the rice barn?

"*Jeed-jeed, Jeed-jeed,*"
A fat gray mouse.

Gray mouse, gray mouse,
don't come squeaking.
Can't you see that
Baby's sleeping?
Gray mouse, gray mouse,
don't you cry,
My baby's sleeping
right nearby.

adford Public Library
30 First St.
adford, VA 24141

Hush!
Who's that leaping
by the well?

"OP-OP, OP-OP,"
A bright green frog.

Green frog, green frog,
don't come leaping.
Can't you see that
Baby's sleeping?

Green frog, green frog,
don't you cry,
My baby's sleeping
right nearby.

Hush!
Who's that sniffling
in the sty?

"UUT-UUT, UUT-UUT,"
   A muddy fat pig.

Fat pig, fat pig,
don't come sniffling.
Can't you see that
Baby's sleeping?
Fat pig, fat pig,
don't you cry,
My baby's sleeping
right nearby.

Hush!
Who's that beeping
by the pond?

"Ghap-ghap, Ghap-ghap,"
A glossy white duck.

White duck, white duck,
don't come beeping.
Can't you see that
Baby's sleeping?
White duck, white duck,
don't you cry,
My baby's sleeping
right nearby.

Hush!
Who's that swinging
from the trees?

"Jiak-jiak! Jiak-jiak!"
A loose-limbed monkey.

Monkey, monkey,
don't come swinging.
Can't you see that
Baby's sleeping?
Monkey, monkey,
don't you cry,
My baby's sleeping
right nearby.

Hush!
Who's that sweeping
at the hay?

"MAAAU, MAAAU,"
An old water buffalo.

Buffalo, buffalo,
don't come sweeping.
Can't you see that
Baby's sleeping?
Buffalo, buffalo,
don't you cry,
My baby's sleeping
right nearby.

Hush!
Who's that shrieking
through the forest?

"HOOM-PRAAA!
        HOOM-PRAAA!"
A great big elephant.

Elephant, elephant,
don't come shrieking.
Can't you see that
Baby's sleeping?

Elephant, elephant,
don't you cry,
My baby's sleeping
right nearby.

Hush!
Is everyone asleep?

All is quiet, all is still.
The mother dozes
at the windowsill.
Nothing's stirring,
not a breeze,
As the moon drifts
up above the trees.
There is no noise now,
there is no sound.

Only Baby's wide awake,
his eyes bright and round.

Radford Public Library
30 First St.
Radford, VA 24141

W24   A 9/11/00
LC 11/21/05   TC 27 C3

last page badly mended 6/05   11-95

E   Ho, Minfong
H   Hush!
c.2

GAYLORD MG